At the Farm

by Cindy Chapman

I see a red hen. What has it got?

I see a pretty cat. It naps a lot.

I see a cow. It has spots.

I see a little rabbit. Hop! Hop! Hop!

I see a pink hog. The hog is fat.

I see a frog hop. Plop! Plop! Plop!

I see a lot on a farm!

Essential Vocabulary

Phonics Words Introduced
got, hog, hop, little, lot, naps, on, pink, plop, pretty, spots

Vocabulary Words
cat, cow, farm, frog, hen, hog, rabbit

Sight Words
a, has, I, is, it, little, on, pretty, red, see, the, what

Farms are fun places to visit—especially if you like animals. In **At the Farm** you will practice your phonics skills while learning about the different kinds of animals that can be seen on a farm.

www.capstoneclassroom.com

ISBN 978-1-62521-977-0